Bentham As It Were

David Johnson

2007
Landy Publishing

ISBN 978-1-872895-74-1

A catalogue record of this book is available from the British Library.

Layout by Sue Clarke
Printed by The Nayler Group, Church, Accrington. Tel: 01254 234247

Landy Publishing have also published:

A Century of Bentham by David Johnson
Bygone Bentham by Joseph Carr
Northward by Anthony Hewitson
Life on the Lancaster Canal by Janet Rigby
The Lancaster Canal in Focus by Janet Rigby
A Portrait of Poulton-le-Fylde by Christine Storey
Preston in Focus by Stephen Sartin
Memories of Colne by Mrs Cryer

A full list of available publications is available from:

Landy Publishing, 'Acorns' 3 Staining Rise, Staining, Blackpool, FY3 0BU
Tel/Fax: 01253 895678 (24hrs), Email: peggie@peggiedobson.wanadoo.co.uk

Cover
The scene on School Hill during Queen Victoria's Diamond Jubilee Celebrations on 22nd June 1897. The picture offers a fine view of the Elementary School and School House. It must feature many of Bentham's most prominent residents. It is worth noting that, stripped of any buildings, School Hill covers a substantial area of land in the centre of the town and that it was an effective centre for public events. *(Photos The Johnson Collection)*

Main Street about 1905. This unique photograph by *A. Horner* captures Bentham Main Street on a hot summer afternoon. At the eastern end of the present day Bentham Club is a sweet or confectionary shop advertising Cadbury's Chocolate and beyond that building, at what is now a redeveloped *Barwise's Bakery*, is Robinson's Plumbers and Cycle Dealers. Opposite on the site of the *Nosebag* is William Richard Vipond's, boot maker and toy dealer's shop whilst further along is John Dickinson's, the drapers. (Also see pages 26 and 29).

INTRODUCTION

Soon after we moved here we realised that, although Bentham may not be the most picturesque place, it is one of the North's best-kept secrets. The friendliness, the support and community spirit impressed us and we are glad we have been able to stay here for the last 33 years.

It has been my privilege to chat to many of Bentham's more elderly residents, some with wonderful memories. In particular I recall one of these characters who always spoke of *'Bentham as it were'* and every time this phrase comes to mind I visualise this elderly gentleman with a prodigious memory sitting on a wall recounting his experiences! Indeed it was at one stage intended to be the title of my 1998 publication but it has resurfaced again in 2007!

This book is an attempt to chronicle some of the changes that have occurred in Bentham over the last 125 years. Looking back it is obvious that High and Low Bentham were two distinct communities. They both had their own mills, churches, schools and social life. I hope through the photographs and text that the story of some aspects of the lives of the two Benthams will emerge from the pages and that both Bentham's long-standing residents and newcomers will enjoy delving into the past.

I have tried to name as many people as possible. I hope those with true Bentham roots will appreciate the difficulty of compiling lists of people who are well known to themselves but not to the author. All I can say is that I have tried my best, they have been checked by real Benthamers and I hope those interested in their family history will find them useful. I have also tried to acknowledge all the sources of my pictures. Every effort has been made not to infringe copyright but if an error has been made I humbly apologise. I also wish to acknowledge the enormous help I have received in compiling this book both from people who lent photographs, those who have furnished me with information and those who have written extracts from their first hand experience. I would like to mention: David Alder, Jenny Cardus, Rhoda, Lily and Albert Coates, Wendy Dowbiggin, Sheila Houghton, Bateman and Margaret Marshall, Peter Marshall, Jim Redfern, Sheila Ward and Bernard Williams for the information they have provided and for checking the draft text. Sadly, Mary Ireland who provided me with many of the more contemporary photographs died in April this year so she will never see her pictures in print. I would like to thank Wendy Dowbiggin, Bateman Marshall and Peter Marshall for their written contributions and my wife Judith for her support, helpful suggestions, proof reading and generally putting up with the mess I make when I am involved in projects like this!!

David Johnson August 2007

3

This sparkling, joyous scene is less formal than the cover picture and features school children, their parents, the Town Band and local dignitaries. It was probably taken from the upper window of the Royal Oak (now Turner's Offices) on 9th August 1902 to mark the coronation of Edward VII. The picture is not perfectly sharp which is unfortunate. It is worth noting that both Queen Victoria's Jubilees and Edward's Coronation were accompanied by glorious sunshine, something that was in short supply for Queen Elizabeth's Jubilees! *(Photo The David Johnson Collection)*

School Hill was the scene for many gatherings and celebrations. This photograph gives a vivid impression of School Hill before it was developed. Note May Cottage to the left of schoolhouse. It was demolished in the 1950s to allow large vehicles access to Robin Lane.
(Photo The Howson Collection)

Queen Victoria's Golden Jubilee held on 21st June 1887

These two unusual and very old photographs illustrate the celebrations held in two different parts of High Bentham. Top left is a picture of a festive crowd gathered in the Wenning Avenue area within the cottages and mill buildings. Residents may not readily recognise the setting because most of the buildings in the picture have been demolished.
(Photo The David Johnson Collection)

Main Street 1887

One of the earliest pictures of this part of the town and it shows that many changes have taken place to the buildings on the southern side of Main Street. In fact that area is difficult to recognise and since this picture was taken there must have been a period of extensive demolition and rebuilding in the area around Tooby's and Ward's shops. The Chip Shop is recognisable as are Grove Cottages in the distance. The street is decked out for Victoria's Golden Jubilee. You can just distinguish one of the many triumphal arches in the distance near Parkinson's Farm. Under this photograph somebody has written the following; *'Main Street Bentham (×) post office on this site and opposite by the horse and trap (√) is where Gilbert and Edith Thornborough's is and next to it is a grocer's shop'.*
(Photo The David Johnson Collection)

These photographs continue the Community Celebration theme. The upper picture is one of two taken from the upper window of Barton house showing the scene on Mount Pleasant during Queen Victoria's Diamond Jubilee Celebration held on 22nd June 1897. The town was bedecked with flags, arches and the street thronged with devoted subjects all dressed in their Sunday Best. There were processions of elaborate floats and the whole event was enhanced by glorious sunny weather. The two washrooms at the end of Collingwood Terrace are clearly visible. Collingwood Terrace was rebuilt in 1900 and the washrooms were then demolished. *(Photo Gordon Clapham)*

The lower picture probably dates from a later period, maybe about 1910. It is likely that it was taken on one of Bentham's Empire Day celebrations. These commenced after Queen Victoria's death in 1901. They were held annually on her birthday (24th May). In 1958 Empire Day was renamed Commonwealth Day. The picture illustrates the use of School Hill as a traditional gathering place. *(Photo The David Johnson Collection)*

Bentham Camp was founded by Joe Hainsworth in 1907 and lasted until 1925. It was located on both banks of the River Wenning on the flat land just to the west of the Wenning Oak and was one of the first holiday camps in Britain.

Joe lived at Rose Bank, Robin Lane. He was an innovator; not only did he found the holiday camp but he also founded Bentham Cinema on the site later occupied by Burndale Residential home, opposite the Primary School. Most of the campers came by train from the Bradford/Leeds area, and were met at the station either by Joe, his brother Walter or his son Reg, and then escorted to the camp. In 1912 a week's stay cost 19/6d. for single men and youths over 15, but ladies and family parties had to pay 21/- per head for "*certain minor amenities*". The price included accommodation and four good meals a day.

Boarded tents for the ladies were located near the water's edge on the southern side of the river, and a compound of larger tents for married couples ("the wilderness") was situated further away from the Wenning with a marquee. Single men campers, other than relatives or specially invited guests, were not allowed in this area, and their tents were on the other side, between the river and the railway line. The two sides were joined by a trestle bridge, but after this was washed away on several occasions, a suspension bridge was built, although this in turn has also gone. *(Photo The David Johnson Collection)*

·A RELIGOUS CEREMONY AT·
— ·BENTHAM CAMP·—
—·" SALAAMING " THE SUN. ·—

"BENTHAM HOLIDAY CAMP" ILLUSTRATED BOOKLET FREE FROM J. HAINSWORTH, BENTHAM, LANCASTER.

An extract from the camp brochure: *'Life at Bentham Camp is pure and simple…we do not make a long list of strict rules and conditions….We have found by experience that those who come to camp, come with the intention of enjoying themselves and helping others to do the same…..You rise each morning early and leave your tent for the morning dip and after a turn of cricket or gymnastics, or a sprint on the bank, you are ready for breakfast, and breakfast is ready for you….after breakfast some will depart on a cycling run, others for a stroll; each one pleases himself and spends the day as he desires. Some lounge about the camp all morning, and sleep during the afternoon; but whatever one elects to do, his time is well spent.'*
(Photo The David Johnson Collection)

-–BATHING AT BENTHAM CAMP-–
BOTH BATHERS (SIMULTANEOUSLY) "EXCUSE ME SIR, BUT THAT'S ONE OF MY COSTUMES —— YOU'VE GOT ON."

BENTHAM HOLIDAY CAMP'' ILLUSTRATED BOOKLET FREE FROM J. HAINSWORTH, BENTHAM, LANCASTER.

An extract from the camp brochure drawn up by Joe Hainsworth, one of Norman Feather's cartoons and a picture of the campers taken in about 1920 at the end of an enjoyable holiday. Norman Feather, according to Joe's son Reg. '*…was a good friend of my father's, and a regular camper. I think he was on the staff of one of our Yorkshire papers…*' The postcards were probably printed prior to 1914. Some feature caving and it is known that the campers sometimes went through Upper Long Churn Cave on Ingleborough as well as the tourist cave at Clapham. The tent shown in the photograph was probably for communal use but the campers' tents were obviously large. In his 1912 brochure Joe states '*..Each tent is arranged to contain three, four, or five bedsteads, which are raised about eighteen inches from the floor, and are very comfortable. An ample supply of good woollen blankets are supplied to each camper, along with pillows and a clean cover….*' (Photos Joe Hainsworth and The David Johnson Collection)

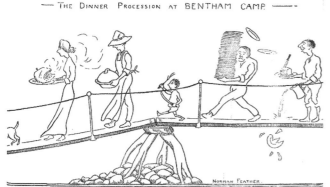

— THE DINNER PROCESSION AT BENTHAM CAMP —

NORMAN FEATHER.

"BENTHAM HOLIDAY CAMP" ILLUSTRATED BOOKLET FREE FROM J. HAINSWORTH, BENTHAM, LANCASTER.

TERMS FOR CAMPING,

Including Sleeping and Four Meals per day. NO EXTRAS.

Any full week (7 days), 17/6 per man. Boys under 15, 15/-.

WEEK-ENDS.

Friday Morning to Monday Night, 10/6 ; to Tuesday Teatime, 12/6.
Saturday Morning to Tuesday Night, 10/6.
Saturday Tea to Sunday Night, 5/-.
Saturday, Dinner or Tea, to Monday Night, 7/6.

3 full days, 10/- ; 4 do., 12/6 ; 5 do.. 15/- ; 6 days count as week

No reduction for boys for any period less than a week.

Tents reserved for 3, 4 or 5 campers, who apply at the same time.
One form will serve for party.

St. John the Baptist Church, Low Bentham is one of the oldest churches in the area. The church dates from Saxon times but it is feasible that its origins go back to the Roman occupation because a Roman road crossed the Wenning just downstream of the present church. As with all buildings, it has experienced its peaks and troughs. The Scots destroyed it after the battle of Bannockburn in 1314: a new church was built in 1340 and it is that tower which we see today. The church was rebuilt in 1822.

The walls were raised by seven metres and three galleries were added together with a new roof. The total cost was £430/10/5d. Because of poor workmanship, a complete rebuild became necessary 54 years later in 1876. The whole building was demolished apart from the tower and the chancel arch and rebuilt to the design of Richard Norman Shaw. The cost escalated to £5,483/5/7d but the work was substantial and has stood the test of time. The top photograph shows the church before its demolition in 1876 and the lower picture the existing post-1876 Norman Shaw building.

(Photos The David Johnson Collection)

The Norman Shaw rebuild of Low Bentham Church was more or less complete by 1879. The photographs dating from this period show a building in a fairly open landscape; there are graves but very few trees. The top picture shows the church during the winter of 1878 or 1879. The main entrance through the church was via the west door and the notice board was fixed to the northern buttress. The hook is still there! The porch was not added until 1881. The lower picture, showing the chancel, and nave dates from the same period. There was no North entrance, simply a window. The original two-manual organ is clearly visible together with the stone tracery which is now concealed by the Lethaby Organ Case. This organ was notable in that it was the first ever to be blown by mechanical power, the mechanism being installed in 1856 before the organ was moved from Leeds to Bentham. The organ was later enlarged and rebuilt to make the organ we see today. *(Photos The David Johnson Collection)*

The six bells of St. John the Baptist, Low Bentham are the heaviest peal of six bells in North Yorkshire. The peal has an aggregate weight of 3 tons 7 cwts 24lbs and the tenor weighs 19cwts 2qtrs 14 lbs. The top photograph shows the bells ready to be rehung in 1877 after two of them had been recast. Interesting aspects of this photograph are a glimpse of the old rectory before it was remodelled by Norman Shaw and the stone sarcophagus dating from the fourteenth century now set into the floor of the chancel.

The lower picture shows the bells being lowered from the tower in October 1926 ready for their journey to Taylor's foundry at Loughborough. They were rehung in January 1927. The whole operation was a saga of difficulties, the two major ones being Taylor's omission to charge for the removal of a mullioned window in the tower to allow them to extract the bells and the other that the foundry was unable to operate normally as they could not obtain coke because of the national coal strike. In the picture are (left to right): ……..?, Percy Low (Rector), Arnold Robinson, Eddy Holmes, …….?, Albert Coates
(Photos The David Johnson Collection)

The Second World War saw an expansion of many voluntary organisations, all of which played their part in the war effort. Here are two pictures of such organisations.

Founder Members of Bentham Fire Brigade taken at Tennants Well Lane about 1940
Left to Right Harold Jackson, Jim Gudgeon, Ken Anderson, P.C. Philpott, John Burton, Philip Harvey
Front Row Arthur Tustin, David Booth, Bert Slinger, C. Holmes, Arthur Slinger
(Photo M. Slinger)

First Aid Post Volunteers and Air Raid Wardens, Low Bentham in about 1944
Back Row Isaac Oldfield, Jim Brayshaw, Mrs L. Walters, Ben Coates, Annie Robinson, Jack Walling, Greta Pierson, John Prince, John Henry Oldfield.

Middle Row Mrs Garrad, Mary Fletcher, Becca Downham, Albert Townley, Mrs. S. Irving, Mrs. Harvey, Alec Wilcock, Mrs. L. Prince, Mrs. M.A. Burrow, Miss E. Prince.
Front Row Norah Carr and Rhoda Coates
(Photo Rhoda Coates)

Henry Slinger used to farm at Low Bottom and part of the farm was an area of level ground adjacent to the river and now included in Riverside Caravan Park. It became known as *'Slinger's Holme'*. It was used occasionally by light aircraft in the 1930s and featured an air circus in 1938. After the Second World War, an army reconnaissance unit camped on the field; they were only there for a short time and had a Tiger Moth. As a way of thanking Henry Slinger for the use of his field they took his portrait on 22nd June 1952. Sadly he died a year later. (*Photo Alice Jackson.*)

Global warming in Bentham?....No!! This picture shows elephants attached to a circus that used to set up behind the Horse and Farrier. They are enjoying a drink from the trough in Bentham Hall Yard in about 1938. (*Photo Bateman Marshall*)

The twentieth century marked an era of massive decline in agriculture, particularly the number of farms and farm workers in the locality. The 1891 census lists 75 farmers in the two parishes. By 1932 there were 68 farms and now, at the onset of the twenty first century only 14 of have survived. There has also been a 75% decline in the number of smallholdings. For example during World War II there were 6 smallholdings between High and Low Bentham. Now there are none. Most of the work was carried out manually and by horsepower. This charming picture shows two farm horses called *'Tommy'* and *'Blossom'* and was probably taken at Green Foot, Low Bentham about 1910. *(Photo Evelyn Willan)*

Robert Cowin lived on School Hill and this photograph, taken in the 1950s shows Norman Stainton of Lairgill with one of Robert Cowin's new ERF lorries. The lorries were designated solely for the transport of T.T. attested cattle. He had 6 vehicles and 6 local drivers. *(Photo Carolyn Simpson)*

The first Bentham Show was held on 14th October 1857. During its history it has missed only fourteen years due to major events such as the wars and foot and mouth disease. The 136th show will be held in September 2007. These two pictures were taken in 1959 on a gloriously sunny day at Millholme, the recreation ground at High Bentham.

The show was held here for many years but other venues have been Big Bank (also known as Brown Cow Field) on the left hand side of Robin Lane where the bungalows are now built), Tennant House Lots, Burrow Barn and Bellfleckers Field (opposite Moons Acre). It has been possible to name two of the three men on the lower picture. They are Percy Kettlewell (left) and John Burton of Ellergill (right).
(Photos The David Johnson Collection)

The top photograph dates from 1921 and shows *'Flashlight'* clearing a fence. He went on to be the First Prize Winner for the year. *(Photo The Howson Collection)*

The lower picture shows the competitors in the fancy dress competition on Fushetts Field in about 1978. Some of the people have been named.

They are (from Left to Right) Salome Titterington (in black), Gaynor South, Fiona Nicholson (waving a bottle), Raymond Heigh (flat cap), Jonathan and Cecil Titterington (Bisto Kids), Joanne Nicholson (white hat). In the background are Mrs Newhouse and Robert Heigh. *(Photo Wendy Heigh)*

Bateman Marshall comments:

"Before the Second World War Bentham had a dramatic society called 'The Bentham Amateur Dramatic Society'. The principal producer was Wilcock Brian Whitaker. Unfortunately it folded during the war but around 1947 Mrs Francis from Austwick started a drama group to read plays. The drama group soon developed a wish to perform and like a phoenix rising from the ashes 'The Bentham Phoenix Players' came into being. The early plays were all of a classical nature, 'Arms and the Man', Shakespeare's 'King John', 'The Importance of Being Earnest', to name a few. The group entered various drama festivals with considerable success, winning at that time the prestigious Skipton drama festival with 'The Hasty Heart'. As the number of members grew (we had almost 100 members) the need for someone in addition to Mrs Francis to produce became evident. Wilcock Whitaker was pressed back into service and produced several plays. An ex-actor working at George Angus he produced 'Worms Eye View', a wartime play and great fun. 'Pygmalion' was another play that stretched the cast. Tom Cardus, Wendy Dowbiggin and Doreen Park were amongst those who all produced plays when Mrs Francis retired. We performed in several halls besides Bentham Town Hall. I remember taking plays to Settle, Skipton, Grassington and Tunstall to name but a few. As television took a hold the number of members began to fall, but they were happy days."

The Phoenix Players Production of *'Blithe Spirit'* 21st-23rd March 1963
Left to Right Helen Guy, Frank Cornthwaite, Wendy Dowbiggin, Dick Elliot, Doris Symonds
(Photo Wendy Dowbiggin)

Bentham Phoenix Players production of *'Bonaventure'* held in Bentham Town Hall 20th, 21st and 22nd November 1952
Left to Right Jessie Lazenby, Tom Cardus, Bateman Marshall, Margaret Marshall, Wilma Fleming, Leslie Reid, Myra Houghton, Phebe Ransley, Wynne Maw, Annie Dawson and Margaret Francis.
(Photo Mrs. J. Cardus)

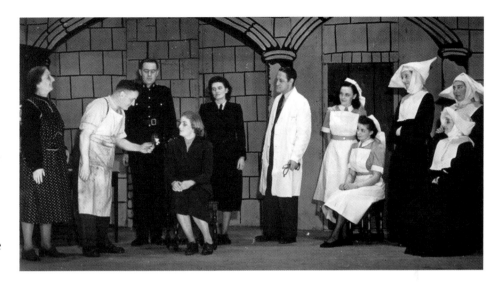

The cast of *'Sailor Beware'* staged in about 1955
Back Row left to right Fred Crossley, Bateman Marshall, Wendy Dowbiggin, Jim Guy, Phyllis Tomlinson (Capstick), John Wright, Winnie Robinson.
Front Row Wendy Young (Reid), Isabel Joel (Johnson)
(Photo Isabel Joel)

It was not until the time the 1870 Education Act came into force that universal education became a possibility in Bentham. Elementary education in Bentham dates back to 1879 but the major part the Victorian building we know today as High Bentham Community Primary School was built in 1896. In the twentieth century there were five headteachers; Mr Charles F. Birchall, Miss Lilian Clark, Miss Nora K. Hazzard, Mr. David Johnson and Mr Jonathan Brown. The two-storey timber extension was constructed between 1966 and 1968 and the ground floor classroom in this extension was opened in January 1993. The two pictures of the building show the large area open for recreation before the

wooden extension was built in 1966 and work in progress constructing the entrance hall in 1967. The portrait shows Miss Nora K. Hazzard, my predecessor, who was the headteacher between 1962 and 1973. She had to cope with all the problems of running a school during the renovations.
(Photo The David Johnson Collection)

For some time the girls and infants were educated separately from the boys. The girls and infants were taught in the old grammar school building, what is now the town library. By 1911 the pattern of education changed and the older girls and boys were educated in the upper building under the headship of Charles Birchall. The infants had their own headteacher (Mary Holmes) and were taught in the old Grammar School. There were two classes with the room being separated by a screen. For part of the early twentieth century the infants, the junior boys and the junior girls had their separate playgrounds. The class photograph, taken about 1922 shows the wall that divided the boys' and girls' playground. *(Photo School Collection)*

The two staff photographs show the staff of the school at this time. The picture with three teachers shows the Infants' staff in 1919. They are Lucy Cumberland (left), Mary Holmes (centre) and Grace Robinson (right). The larger group shows the junior school teachers in 1919. They are; back row left to right Annie Grisedale, Charles Frederick Birchall, Annie Morphet. Front row Mary Birchall (Charles Birchall's wife) and Margaret Atkinson. (Photos Kathy Townson)

High Bentham Girls and Infants Class 1911
Back Row ....?, Maggie Towler, Mary Jackson, Olive Newhouse, Dorothy Harrison, Phoebe Bibby, Mary Sandham, Lizzie Thompson, Grace Alston.
Third Row Miss Grace Robinson, Annie Ammatt, Lizzie Brennand, Edith Taylor, Lizzie Wilkinson, Eliza Hinchcliffe, Annie Ellershaw, Peggy Proctor, Maggie Charnley, Miss M. Holmes.

Second Row Marjorie Holmes, Annie Bowker, Bessie Clapham, Emily P. Wrathall, Mary Phillipson, Lizzie Gudgeon, Kathleen Harrison.
Front Row Addie Macdonald, Alice Foster, Lily Jackson, Maggie Leeming, Maud Tattersall.
(Photo The David Johnson Collection)

High Bentham C.P. School 1935
Fourth Row Walter Newhouse, Ken Guy, Brian Taylor, Brian Metcalfe, Ken .....?, Leslie Jackson, ...?, Reg Richardson, ...? Ernest Denby.
Third Row ....?, Margery Caton, Margaret West, Gwen Sanderson, Audey Batty, Jean Parker, Evelyn Wrathall, ...? Donnelly, Linda Foster, Clara Jenkinson.
Second Row ....?, William Foster, Mary Mudd, Audrey Thompson, Audrey Jackson, Isabel Johnson, Doreen Crawford, Maureen Willan, ...? Smith, Tom Proctor.
Front Row Edgar Leak, David Greenep, ...? (Photo Isabel Joel)

22

High Bentham Primary School 1954
Back Row Miss Elsie Wilshaw, Ken Brownsord, Colin Newhouse, Roger Metcalfe, Stuart Holding, Chris Reid, Ron Hoggarth, Barry Slinger.
Next to the Back Row Peter Thompson, David McKenna, Maurice Bowker, Peter Watson, Peter O'Neil, Robin Segger, John Emmott, Jimmy Noon, Douglas Haig.
Next to Front Row Susan Wilson, Pauline Fleming, Muriel Wilkinson, Carol Noble, Elizabeth Brown, Margaret Jackson, Barbara Newhouse, Jean Coates, Jean Shuttleworth, June Slinger, Stephany Reid.
Front Row Margaret Smith, Pat Campbell, Sheena Rigg, Joyce Cowgill, Deidre Leak, Susan Yates, Norma Stainton, Linda Preston. *(Photo School Collection)*

High Bentham Primary School 1960
Back Row (left to right) David Gudgeon, Steven Fry, Andrew Bradley, Philip Park, Mike Brown.
Middle Row Rupert Townson, Anthony Bateson, Dennis Haigh, Stanley Wilkinson, Richard Greenep, Terry Newhouse, Dennis Richards, Bernard Williams.
Front Row Janet Pilling, Susan Foster, Maureen Taylor, Pat Robinson, Kathryn Yates, Marion Trew, Christine Jowett, Grace Keenan, Marian Jackson, Susan Johnson, Barbara Wilcock
(Photo Margaret Hayton)

Foster's was a prominent bakery and grocers shop on the corner of Main Street and Robin Lane. It occupied the site now taken by the Cooperative Stores. The Foster family lived at Barton House. The photographs were taken about 1900 and show Barton House, the family home, a view looking east towards Mount Pleasant and another looking west towards the Black Bull. The man in the white apron is probably James Foster, the manager. They had a bake-house behind the shop and made bread and cakes. They also sold dairy produce and had a café that served lunches to farmers on market day. In the 1930s the business had a

fleet of vans which delivered to customers as far away as Clapham, Austwick and other outlying areas. The vans had to be especially narrow to get to the back of the shop to load.
(Photos E. Duesbury, Mr and Mrs W. Foster)

'Hash Browns' is a relatively modern name for what was once known as 'Brown and Whittakers'. It was originally Marshall's Joiners, Cabinet Makers and Undertakers but Thomas Brown and Wilcock Brian Whittaker bought the business in 1909 from Thomas Marshall. In the 1930s part of the building was Phillipson's clock and watch shop, then it was Howson's flower and fruit shop for a short period before the entire building was given over to Brown and Whittaker's business. The photograph of the shop, taken in about 1900, shows goods being hoisted into the building from a horse and cart. The accompanying advertisements provide much information about the business.

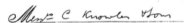

BENTHAM,   *Midsummer* 189⁴

Mess C Knowles & Son

Bought of THOMAS MARSHALL,
Complete House Furnisher.

BRASS AND IRON BEDSTEADS, SPRING, HAIR, AND STRAW MATTRASSES, FEATHER AND FLOCK BEDS.

CARPETS, LINOLEUMS, AND FLOOR OIL CLOTHS.

AGENT FOR THE END OVER END, BARREL AND OTHER CHURNS.

WASHING AND WRINGING MACHINES, SEWING MACHINES, Etc.

FUNERALS FURNISHED.

TERMS :

The other photographs concentrate on the funeral business. The photographs taken about 1980 show Eric Brown and Tony Lamb in the firm's hearse and one of their employees, Jimmy Macdonald, in his *working clothes*. (*Photos Bateman Marshall and Bill Hinde*)

PHILLIPSON,
Watch & Clock Maker, Jeweller, &c.,
- Main Street. Bentham.

Fancy Goods suitable for Presents.

Best Non-crazing
DINNER WARE.

CHINA TEA SETS leadless glaze

Special HERALDIC CHINA for Collectors.

'The Nose Bag' coffee shop and cafe was once a shoe shop. During the 1920s the shop belonged to William Richard Vipond but by 1936 ownership had been bought by J. M Parker and Sons and subsequently to Brian *('Curly')* and Marian Parker until the 1980s.

These splendid photographs show the Vipond family posing outside their shop about 1923; a display of slippers and shoes from the early 1920s and the shop window as on 29th July 1981 decorated to mark the wedding of Diana and Prince Charles. *(Photos F.E.Hewitt)*

These two pictures give a vivid impression of quieter streets in Bentham. The picture with an oval frame is the earlier of the two and probably dates from about 1890. It was in the base of a tray covered by glass and was the property of Betsy Marriott of Police Yard. At some stage the glass had been cracked and as it was not possible to remove the picture, it has been repaired digitally. It is unusual in that it shows Saul's and Wilcock's shops on the left; they predated Central Buildings (now Bentham Sports) built in 1906. *(Photo B. Marriott)*

The other picture dates from about 1900. The shop with the blind extended is Foster's (see page 24). The shop nearest the left hand side of the picture was Garlick's, a ladies and gentlemens' outfitters which was founded in 1872 by George Wade Garlick and closed in 1959. In its early days the firm employed 15 people and toured as far as Kirkby Lonsdale and Tosside collecting and delivering garments.

The board tucked away in the corner above and behind the two girls advertises Parrington's boot and shoe business. It was passed down the Parrington family until it was sold to Ken and Peggy Duke in 1947. Later Eddie and Winnie Gill took over the shoe shop but it is now a private dwelling. *(Photo The Howson Collection)*

It isn't often that dramas or catastrophes occur in Bentham, thank heavens, but two occurred in Main Street in the same year. Kersey's Garage collapsed on 9th October 1981 and just two months later, in December, a fire broke out at the Horse and Farrier. These incidents were captured on camera by *Mary Ireland*. Following these events the Spar supermarket chain bought and developed the site of the garage. A squash court was opened at The Horse and Farrier about 1982.

The Barwise family have traded as bakers and confectioners at their shop in Main Street since March 1953. Bernard bought the business, once known as the *'Beehive Café'*, from the Eastham family but before that the building had a long and complicated history. Similar to many buildings in Main Street it was probably once a farmhouse. Pre-World War II, the shop belonged to Mrs Kershaw who was known for baking large sheets of oatcake one took home to dry. During the 1939-45 war the Beehive belonged to the Proctors. There was a tiny shop and house adjacent to Barwise's and it is now part of the Conservative Club. Pre-war and shortly afterwards it was Cooper's, a cobbler's shop, and later Leslie Reid's second hand furniture and bric a brac shop after his main shop (now *'Independent Financial Advisors Choices'*) burnt down in February 1953.

The pictures show Bernard proudly displaying a tray of bread *(Photo Bill Hinde)* and a view of Main Street about 1915 including the Beehive Café; with the blind shielding the baking from the mid-day sun. *(Photo A. Horner)*

Bentham station was originally built in the Midland Railway *'Gothic'* style. In 1923 the company became part of the London, Midland and Scottish Railway Company. The station was rebuilt, as in the picture on the right, in the early 1950s soon after the LMS Railway had become a part of the nationalised British Railways. Seen here is locomotive no. 43295 working hard pulling a goods train towards Leeds on 12th May 1956. The Midland Railway built over 300 of these engines from 1885 onwards. *(Photo John Hammond)*

The railway first came to Bentham with the formation of the *'Little'* North Western Railway in 1850. Within a couple of years it was leased to the Midland Railway and this view, looking east, shows Bentham Station about 1910. The Bentham Gas Company was founded in 1884 and one of the two floating gasholders is just discernible below and to the left of the mill chimney. The picture is interesting because it is a very early picture of the Angus complex that was built about 1908. The chimney, drying tower and some other buildings are clearly visible. The buildings in the foreground are a stoneyard. At an earlier date this plot of land was a coal yard but later became the *'Pennine Boarding Kennels'* belonging to James Robinson. The lattice bridge is visible in the distance with sidings on each side of the line; one set running into the Angus factory and another on the left serving Pye's Corn Mill and warehouse. All goods from Angus' left the factory by rail until the late 1950s. *(Photo W.P. Howson) Information provided by Peter Marshall, Bateman Marshall and Jim Redfern.*

A Midland Railway 0-6-0 locomotive (No. 564) awaits its departure signal, with its crew of two and a couple of local porters. The engine was built in the early 1880s to the design of Matthew Kirtley. *(Photo E. Etherington)*

Bentham Station staff are seen here on a group photograph c. 1900. The Midland Railway horsebox is beside the cattle pens that were located at that time behind the main station buildings. The 1881 census lists Benjamin Ash, aged 36, as Station Master, and other railway employees were three signalmen, three porters, three platelayers, a drayman, a timber loader and fourteen labourers. *(Photo Sheila Hodgson), text by Peter Marshall*

This wintry scene, taken in December 1888, is one of our earliest views of Bentham. You will notice there are no buildings on the west side of the road. The shops on the left extended only as far as the Co-operative Society buildings and the block beyond Jordan's the solicitors had yet to be built. The original entrance to Grove Hill is clearly visible. The west side of the road below what is now Wood's Accountants was lined with magnificent trees. These have sadly gone, but clues to their existence (and species) can be found in the house names below the National Westminster Bank, e.g. *Chestnut House and Elm House (Photo the David Johnson collection)*

The expansion of Station Road (originally *'Slaidburn Road'*) probably commenced from the Black Bull on one side of the road and The Kings Arms on the western side and worked down the hill towards the railway (page 50). The earliest post offices were located in Main Street on the site of what is now the fish and chip shop and

then probably Armstrong's hardware shop. As shown in the 1890 photograph by the presence of the postmaster it had then moved to the southern end of the block occupied today by Wood's the accountants. Eventually the building was used by Hargreaves the accountants and then the Midland Bank before finally assuming its current use by Woods the accountants. Note that Station Road was once quite an elegant tree-lined road with very few houses or shops, and that Wood's was the last building on the southern side of the street at this time. (*Photos I. Wood*)

Tom Guy cutting Francis *'Fran'* Forster's hair. *(Photo Bill Hinde).* The Forster family owned what is now the Sue Ryder shop. It was originally Mrs Marshall's newsagents, toyshop and stationers before the Forster family purchased it and continued the business. Fran's father was a photographer, and Fran, who was a good all-round sportsman, continued the business until the 1990s. He had a small lending library and always stocked a wide range of goods. The shop is clearly visible on the photograph of Station Road taken about 1930. It is just to the right of what is now the National Westminster Bank. *(Photo The David Johnson Collection)*

Bottom right is the stained glass decoration in the door of Cogill's workshop. The building has recently been demolished. *(Photo Mary Ireland)*

It can be seen that the Wenning Bridge that preceded the present utilitarian structure was a bridge of charm and elegance completely in keeping with its surroundings. This beautiful Edwardian photograph taken about 1906 portrays the bridge on a sleepy summer day. There is time and space to fish, stand around in the road and chat and for children to play in safety. Far removed from the frenzied activity of the twenty first century! *(Photo A. Horner)*

The bridge collapsed at 7.10 a.m. on 13th December 1964. The tragedy was caused because the weir, designed to divert water into Wenning Silks millrace, had been allowed to deteriorate to such an extent that floodwaters were able to breach it and the sudden increase in the current swept away the bridge. The photograph taken in about 1910 shows the weir, the head of water, the mill and the sluice gates. *(Photo The Howson Collection)*

This photograph taken on 13th December 1964 looking upstream from the western side of the bridge shows the devastation created following the collapse of the weir.
(Photo Cliff Humphries)

After the collapse a Bailey bridge was erected up stream of the old bridge from the site of the old bathing hut to a point on Richard Turner's side. Rebuilding commenced on 2nd May 1966 and the new bridge was officially opened on 5th May 1968. This photograph was taken in March 1968 just before the bridge was opened.
(Photo Mrs P. Cowgill)

'The Big Stone' has been a source of interest and wonder to visitors and locals alike for many years. We know nothing about the group portrayed in the photograph except that they possibly arrived on one or two charabancs. The picture was probably taken about 1910. *(Photo The David Johnson Collection)*

The cartoon was one of a series of postcards drawn by Norman Feather and sold at the Bentham Camp (see page 9). Joe Hainsworth used the cards as an effective and light-hearted advertising tool to attract more visitors to the camp. *(Photo The David Johnson Collection)*

HOW THEY WOO AT BENTHAM.
THE BIG STONE AT SUNRISE.

This aerial view of Ford Ayrton Silk Mill at Low Bentham was taken in the 1950s. You can see the mill in its heyday. The angled skylights were designed to provide maximum light for the workers. The mill employees used the allotments further along Mill Lane. In the bottom left hand corner one can discern the geometric pattern of the rose gardens. The 'cut' (the millrace) is clearly visible in the top left hand corner of the picture. It was in this millrace that Mrs Gill, the wife of the Headmaster at Bentham Grammar School, taught the boys to swim in the 1920s and 1930s.
(Photo The David Johnson collection)

The Fords were a philanthropic Quaker family who valued their workforce. The lower picture shows the opening of the rose garden. The Fords created this rose garden and the footbridge, linking it to the mill in 1929 to mark the fiftieth anniversary of the business moving to Bentham. The footbridge also provided the workforce with a direct route between the mill and the village. *(Photo Mary Parker)*

In a previous book *'A Century of Bentham'* I was able to publish two pictures of a boiler being delivered to the Ford, Ayrton Silk Mill. It appears that these pictures were part of a series illustrating the whole operation. The other part of the set has now come to light. They confirm that Hewitt and Kellet of Bradford were the manufacturers. The new photographs, shown here, reveal that two boilers were delivered at the same time and that they were fitted into a new boiler house designed by Thomas Benson Pease Ford in about 1907. *(Photos R. Currie)*

This view shows the allotments cultivated by the mill's employees. It was taken from the bank overlooking the mill about 1942. Every inch is under cultivation, a response to the need to produce as much food as possible during the war. *(Photo M. Hayton)*

Ford, Ayrton's Silk Mill closed in 1970. It had declined from its former proud state to sad neglect by the time of its demolition in the Spring of 2004. The mill chimney was demolished on 16th April of that year. Russell Armer Ltd has now developed the land for houses, apartments and light industrial use. The gable end of Rose Cottages can be seen in the middle distance, a vista unseen for 200 years and probably remaining hidden from view for another two centuries! *(Photos David Johnson and R. Currie)*

The quarry at Lairgill provided sand for the ironworks at Carnforth. This fine picture shows the quarry before the following events occurred as reported by *'The Craven Herald'* 27th December 1907: *"The sand quarry at Lairgill was about finished when Lairgill Beck broke through in November and flooded them out, and a new one had to be found. Mr Barton of the Carnforth Iron Works purchased the field behind the Plough Inn* (now Plough Cottage) *and a new quarry was at once opened, and a road made direct to the station"'* (Photo Gordon Clapham)

Johnny Coulam, in an interview for *'The Craven Herald'* 4th October 1929 recalled: *"Up Springfield there was nothing, apart from the old Lairgill Quarry, out of which the late Mr Armstrong obtained sand, the first cartload of which Mr Coulam helped to tip. In the bottom, hard by the quarry, stood a farmhouse which was demolished years ago."*

In 1904 George Angus & Co. Ltd leased the bleach works at the High Bentham Mill (the Wenning Avenue complex) from the Bentham Hemp Company (part of The Hemp and Cordage Co. Ltd). The Angus firm was based in Newcastle but came to Bentham in 1907 because of the high reputation of a skilled workforce in weaving canvas hose and woven belts. The industry thrived in Bentham because the damp climate and soft water were suitable for the production of textiles, such as linen. In the December of 1907 the *'Craven Herald'* commented…*'Angus and Co. have, during the back end, been spending about £10,000 in the erection of a new mill in the Victoria Field behind the Vicarage….Great hopes are entertained of the project which will necessitate the employment of considerably more workpeople than their old works. Cottage property is now difficult to get. Not a single cottage is to be found empty in Bentham.'*

The photograph on the left shows the early excavation for the mill with the old vicarage in the far distance. This building is now part of the Kidde Complex. A rare view of the early mill is to be found on page 30. *(Photo The Kidde Collection)*

This picture shows the reinforced rubber lining department in the 1950s. On the picture are: Bill Mossop, Charlie Barker, Les West, Jack Pedder, Maurice Metcalfe, Vince Slinger, Dick Leek and Dick Rucastle. *(Photo The Kidde Collection)*

Angus Thermoflex Department about 1955. This department made fireproof gloves woven from asbestos string. Samples can be seen hanging from the wall.
Near Side Left to Right Mrs Foster, Jean Robinson,
Far Side Left to Right Margaret Seggar, Fanny Cooper and Margaret Maudsley.
(Photo The Kidde collection)

In about 1954 the B.B.C. programme *'Workers' Playtime'* visited Angus. The production was held in Bentham Town Hall and featured Eve Boswell. In the photograph John Cockshott (Works Manager) is on her right and Derek Roy (comedian) is on her left. Eve was born Eva Keleti in Budapest, Hungary in 1924. She was a singer of popular songs in the 1950s. She did much touring with Derek Roy and Tommy Cooper. She was able to sing in several languages, was an accomplished pianist and a multi-instrumentalist. Her hit-parade bestsellers were *'Sugar Bush'* and *'Pickin' a Chicken'*.
(Photo The Kidde Collection)

Employees are the backbone of any business and on the next two pages there is a record of some workers at Angus' during the 1950s and 1960s. At its peak the factory had in the region of five or six hundred employees many of whom were bussed in from Lancaster and the surrounding area. The factory was, and still is, renowned for its production of fire-fighting equipment such as fire hose, fire extinguishers, foam and foam generators. Today, lorries visit Bentham from all corners of Europe to collect and deliver its products.

Machine Shop Personnel, 1954
Back Row Arthur Watkinson, Gerald Ely, Michael Kinrade, Tony Davey, Sam Dobbin, Ted Holmes, Alan Bowers, Frank Eldon and Jack Devitt
Seated Reg McKenna, Alf Kaulsbarsch, Frank Wheildon, Ted Kennedy, Harry Mackay, Stan Kinrade, Bert Foster and Wilf Wilson
Front Sam Salt, Freddie Carter and Bert Gott

Hose Finishing Personnel, 1957
Left to Right Frank Parkinson, John Clark, Joe West, Harold Lister, Robert Thompson, Bill Ellershaw, Alf Hallard, Godfrey Harrison, Stan Childs, Joe Chapman, Fred Smith, Bill Staveley, Jimmy Staveley, Raymond Guy and Billy Fleming.
(Photos The Kidde Collection)

43

Canteen Staff 1955
The canteen operated during the daytime shifts and fed the workers under the supervision of Connie Grimshaw, the manageress.
Back Row Mrs. Evans, Anna Hebblethwaite, Mrs. Reid, Mrs. Hoop, Florrie Emmott, Mary Bibby.
Seated Mrs. Childs, Edith Campbell, Connie Grimshaw, Margaret Ashton, Marian Aitken.
(Photo The Kidde Collection)

Canteen Staff 1964
Back Row Jenny Tomlinson, Mary Clark, Georgina Yates, Heather Todd, Edie Ross, Lillian Smith
Front Row Frances Childs, Connie Grimshaw, Nancy Hoop, Dorothy Franklin
(Photo The Kidde Collection)

Wenning Silks occupied the buildings at High Mill. The complex stretched along the Eastern Side of Wenning Avenue from Slaidburn Road to the bleach works (where the caravan site is situated today). The mill changed hands several times before being bought by the Kattan family in 1931. They wove artificial silk as opposed to the natural silk produced by the Ford, Ayrton Mill at Low Bentham. The pictures illustrate some of the processes.

KATTAN'S WENNING SILK MILLS, BENTHAM.

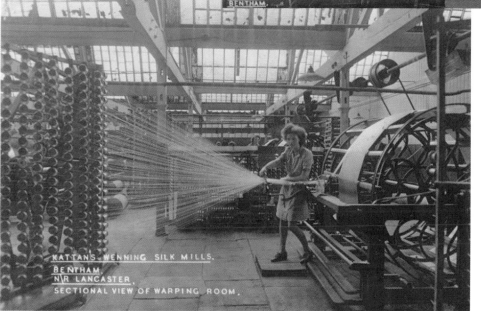

KATTAN'S WENNING SILK MILLS.
BENTHAM,
N/R LANCASTER,
SECTIONAL VIEW OF WARPING ROOM.

The top picture shows the weaving shed with its looms and below is the warping room in the 1960s. The mill closed in 1976 when there were only 60 employees on its books, a sad comparison to a century earlier when it had employed seven or eight hundred people! *(Photos Muriel Humphries)*

Pye's Mill, near the railway station was once a corn mill and later an outlet for animal food and fertilizers used locally on the farms. The top photograph taken in 1957 shows a Pye's trip to Bibby's at Liverpool. Bibby's had a broad range of interests including the production of animal feed. Fred Cook

organized the trips. Because of the way the group is arranged it is difficult to name people in the normal way but amongst those on the picture are: Robert Haythornthwaite, Alan Wills, Fred Cook, Ted Dawson, John Atkinson, Harry Staveley, Jim Hope, Ronnie Rushton, ? Preece, Jim Burrow and John Wilman *(Photo Mary Taylor)*

The lower photograph shows a Fred Richards coach going to The Cross Streets public house near Austwick in 1946. Fred owned a small haulage and coach business in Bentham
Back Row John Hill, Jim Wrathall, Norman Stainton, Billie Magoolagan, Jim Nash
Front Row Fred

Richards, Norman Fry, Ronnie Guy, Hubert Houghton, George Burrow, Ruben Wilcock, 'Pom' John Clark, Arthur Ellershaw. *(Photo Bernard Ellershaw)*

Wendy Dowbiggin, Leader in Charge, writes:

'Bentham Youth Club was held in the Community Centre in the 1970s when these photos were taken and it is still held there today. We had a variety of concerts for several years around Christmas time when  *we performed for the OAPs in the town. They were wonderful times, the young people danced, sang and performed little plays and sometimes they wrote them. I helped with the lines and the costumes. I remember Eric Shuttleworth was MC and several youngsters you see on the photographs still live in the town today; some are married. Nick and Joanne Houghton (Carter), Brian and Dawn Carter (Thornton), Diane Hilton (Pennington), Bob Lister, Ernie Close, Beverley Wilcock (Carter), Ann Collins (Cochrane) and Marina Harrison (Percy). Also on the photograph are Edward Ely, Vanessa Couling, Jayne Philipson, Angela Slinger, Janet Frost, Mark and Paul Hudson and Christine Aitken. Good days!'*

On the lower picture are:
Back Row Jayne Philipson (at the extreme back on the right), Mark Hudson, Bob Lister, Paul Hudson, Nicholas Houghton.
Middle Row Suzanne Pedley, Sharon Ely, Janet Frost, Vanessa Couling, Dawn Thornton, Wendy Dowbiggin
Front Row Diane Pennington, Joanne Carter, Amanda Humphreys, Pippa Shaw, Joanne Mattinson.
(Photos by M. Ireland)

'Nellie Luke's Dancing school must conjure up lots of memories. Lots of little and big girls danced for Nellie! Her pantomimes and concerts were known throughout the district. Much of the money was raised for the R.N.I.B. Brian Taylor of Green Smithy was in the pantos and shows for 21 years starting in 1940. Nellie came to Bentham with Billy Fuller and Coral Curtis, better known as 'Swifty' and 'Nanna'. They all lived in the corner of Cleveland Square (now the car park and market place). The house was regularly full of costumes being made for one of the shows. In later years father and son Harry and Roy Wilkinson formed the comedy act but before them there were the well known personalities of Billy Smith and Walter Ely who starred in Arthur Patrickson's Cricket Concerts which were the highlights of the year.'

Roy (on the left) and Harry Wilkinson

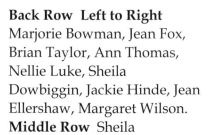

Back Row Left to Right
Marjorie Bowman, Jean Fox, Brian Taylor, Ann Thomas, Nellie Luke, Sheila Dowbiggin, Jackie Hinde, Jean Ellershaw, Margaret Wilson.
Middle Row Sheila Hutchinson, Kathleen Ellershaw, Maureen Lyn, Judith Brownsord, Joan Hutchinson, Jane Reid, Winifred Newhouse, Doreen Ellershaw
Front Row Judith Wellington, Pat Campbell, Sheila Bell, Ann Magoolagan, Jill Symonds, Susan Yates, Sheena Rigg, Hilary Summers.
(Article by Wendy Dowbiggin,. Photos The David Johnson Collection)

'Dancing classes were held in the ballroom of the Town Hall and there were many stars, some of whom still reside in Bentham; Kathleen Ellershaw (Sharples), Sheila Hutchinson (Houghton), Margaret Tierney (Smith), Susan Parnell (Smith), Ann Fleming (Thomas), and Sheila Holmes (Dowbiggin). Ann and Sheila were 'Carroll Levis Discoveries'. The pantos were performed locally and also went on tour as 'Swifty's Gang'. Brian Taylor was an

excellent singer trained by Kathy Parker who was married to Reg Ward. They had a band that played at Nellie Luke's events. Their son Reg took over after his father and played the drums for many years. Reg still lives in Bentham and together with Sheila is the owner of the sweet shop in the Main Street. The late Johnny Wright took part in some of the shows and was a good ballad singer. Also in the town was a rival dance class run by Barbara Jackson who was a well known dancer. Many young girls went to her classes and performed in her shows. Barbara Lipscombe (Jackson) continued with dancing all her working life.'

Left to Right Cathryn Yates, Eileen Ellershaw, Ingrid Bell, Margaret Smith, Brenda Pye, Doris Symonds, Mary Oldfield, Gwen Henderson, Marian Chamberlain.

Back Row Left to Right Sheila Dowbiggin, Maureen Lyn, Reg Ward, Joan Hutchinson, Sheena Rigg, John Symonds, Sheila Hutchinson, Kathleen Ellershaw, Judith Wellington, Carol Curtis, Doreen Ellershaw, Brian Taylor, Kathy Ward, Roy Wilkinson, Ann Thomas, Nellie Luke.
Middle Row Heather Slee, Sarah Roe, ? Field, Ann Hutchinson,

Eileen Ellershaw, Ann Magoolagan, Claire Whitford, ...?, Christine Staveley, Susan Yates, Margaret Smith,
Front Row *(line with dark dresses)* Ann Staveley, Valerie Preston, Susan Johnson, Susan Foster, ? Field, Nan Donaldson, Sheila Bell, Hilary Summers, Kathryn Yates
(Article by W. Dowbiggin, Photos The David Johnson Collection)

The King's Arms Hotel was extensive and occupied the entire block that is now the HSBC Bank and Amy's Hairdressers. It also took in the length of buildings along the east side of King Street as far as the 'Looking Well' building. George Fox is thought to have lodged here overnight on his way, as a prisoner, from Lancaster to Scarborough Castle. Later it became Knowles and Sons Grocers shop. The building mentioned earlier on the east side of the street was the stables for the hotel. For a while the Dalesman Publishing Company had an office on the top floor. In the 1980s Bernard Armstrong decided to open a garden centre in these buildings. On clearing the old stables he discovered numerous stoneware jars and bottles (some Burton Stoneware) that had been deposited there by the Knowles. The photographs show the street before it was changed *(Photo Mary Ireland)* and Bernard Armstrong outside the garden centre *(Photo Bill Hinde)*. After several years the garden centre closed and it was occupied by the 'Looking Well' until it moved into its current premises. Sadly Bernard, a successful business man and popular character, died in 2005.

Between May 1970 and 1998, Bernard Wildman ran a food and freezer centre at the end of King Street. This site has now been purchased and developed by Pioneer Projects (*The Looking Well*). This building is Georgian, dating back to the end of the eighteenth century and was almost certainly built as a house. The side facing towards Station Road bears evidence of a central door and windows. Access was probably directly from the house onto Slaidburn Road because the shops and offices, which now line the road, had not been built. More recently it became a provender warehouse for Lunesdale Farmers. There was a hoist to raise and lower grain through its double doors. The photographs show King Street with the freezer centre sign before the east side was converted into a garden centre (*Photo Mary Ireland*), and Bernard Wildman standing outside the doors of the freezer centre (*Photo Bill Hinde*)

The Ewecross Historical Society was founded in 1968 and still thrives today. The photograph was taken in 1975 and shows (left to right): Edward Huddleston, John Wilson, Mary Taylor, Nellie Dowbiggin, Annie Cowgill and Clifford Murphy. They are looking at some historical artifacts gathered together for an exhibition in Bentham Town Hall. The Ewecross Historical Society meets on the last Monday evening of the month between September and March. There is also the Ingleborough Archaeology Society that meets on the third Monday evening of the month at the Ingleborough Community Centre.

The photograph below shows members on a walk in 1977 at Clintsfield. They are left to right: Brian Ireland, Nellie Dowbiggin, Mrs. Hartley, Muriel Humphries, ……..?, Cliff Humphries, Mr Bassington (at front in white shirt), John Wilson, Mrs. Hall (partially in view) and Edward Huddleston. *(Photos Mary Taylor)*

Dr. Leslie Dowell on his waste paper round. He and his wife Dr. Elizabeth were deeply involved in community life. Leslie was the senior partner of the Bentham Practice and Dr. Elizabeth was President of the Craven N.S.P.C.C. and Chair of the Bentham Branch that she started in the late 1950s. They were both Magistrates and town councilors. Dr Dowell and Mary Ireland started the waste paper collection to raise funds for the *'Arthritis and Rheumatism Council'* but in 1990 the N.S.P.C.C. took over the project. The surgery was based at Bentham Lodge and moved to its present location about 1970. *(Photo Mary Ireland)*

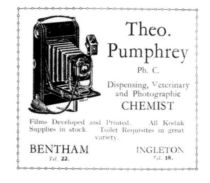

Theo. Pumphrey
Ph. C.

Dispensing, Veterinary and Photographic
CHEMIST

Films Developed and Printed.   All Kodak Supplies in stock.   Toilet Requisites in great variety.

BENTHAM   INGLETON
Tel. 22.   Tel. 18.

The daughter of a policeman, Annie Cowgill was born in Wythenshawe, Manchester, but moved to Bentham when she was two years old. When her mother (Mrs Kearton) was widowed she opened a dressmaking and millinery shop on Station Road (now *The Gallery*), between the butcher's and the bank. She attended Settle Girls High School before training as a teacher at Bingley College. After qualifying, she taught throughout the district. She married Eric Dawson, a railway signalman but she was widowed in her forties and later married Thomas Cowgill. She had a strong interest in Bentham. She was a member of the Ewecross Historical Society, the Women's Institute, the Drama Group and a manager at the Primary School. She played an active part in all these organizations but illness overtook her and she moved to the Isle of Man to be near her family. She died in 1985. *(Photo Mary Ireland)*

Wendy Dowbiggin writes:

'Nellie Dowbiggin was born in Wray in 1910, daughter of Jim and Alice Guy. They moved to Duke Street in Bentham shortly after Nellie's birth and when she married Jim Dowbiggin they made their home at No 4 Pinewood where her daughter, Wendy, lives today. Nellie worked in many shops in the town after her marriage and when her daughter had started school. She was employed at Alice Wilkinson's lingerie shop (now the Co-op Chemist), Shuttleworth's Grocery (now Andrew Errington's Print Shop) and latterly at Frost's Bakers (now Oakroyd Bakery)…Nellie started her career as a confectioner at the Co-op Café (now the flats on Station Road next to Derek Jordan the solicitor).

Her main interest was the W.I. and she was President for several years. She entered Bentham Show and was on the Handicraft Committee. She was also a keen member of the Ewecross Historical Society and was a founder member along with Annie Cowgill. She was the local reporter for the 'Lancaster Guardian', 'Craven Herald' and 'Westmorland Gazette', a job her husband Jim had and now her daughter Wendy has – nothing new under the sun! Nellie died in May 1975' (Photo by M. Ireland)

Hannah Robinson was born in 1892 and died at the age of 103 on January 23rd 1995. The photograph was taken by Mary Ireland to mark her 100th birthday. She was one of the oldest inhabitants of Bentham and had a long, busy life. She worked in the sewing room at the Angus factory until she retired in the 1950s. *(Photo M. Ireland)*

For many years the Slinger family held coffee mornings at Tennant Well House as a way of raising funds for St. Margaret's Church. The furniture for the garden party had to be carried from the ' *Legion Hut*'. If the weather was poor the coffee mornings were held in the Town Hall. Social events are still a feature of summer months. These pictures show the 1980 event in full swing.

Those featured in the top picture are: (Left to Right) Dorothy Hurtley, Dora Smith, Evelyn Willan, Charles Harrison, and (standing) Freda and Albert Coates.

In the bottom picture are: (Left to Right) Dora Smith, Betsy Marriot, Mary Bowker, Hannah Robinson, Alice Brownsord, Sheree and Elsie Dawson. *(Photos Mary Ireland)*

'Badminton was played in the old Wenning Hall before the war. There were two clubs, 'Bentham Badminton Club' and 'Wenning Badminton Club'. When the improved Town Hall was opened in 1940, both clubs moved in. The Bentham Badminton Club played social badminton and it eventually folded around 2000. The Wenning Club played competitively, first in a local league and later in the Lancaster League. Under Desmond Redhead's coaching, the standard improved and it was not long before they were winning at national level. At one time the club had no less than seven All England Champions at Junior level. Kathleen Redhead was rated fourth in the country at senior level. She played for England, as did Carl Wood, Paul Wood, Gary Scott and Susan Parker at Junior level. Bob Capstick played for Yorkshire and Lynva Russell and Kathleen Redhead were national schools champions. The club featured on television and in the national newspapers. Sadly the club no longer exists.'
These photographs were loaned by Desmond Redhead and were taken in the 1960s.
(Text by Bateman Marshall)

Back Row Frannie Forster, Bateman Marshall (chairman), Ian Taylor, Sid Hogg, Bobby Capstick
Front Row Carol Leak, Irene Redhead, Katie Carr

Back Row Desmond Redhead, Frannie Forster, Carol Leak, Christine Ralston, Ann Staveley, Katie Carr
Front Row Terry Newhouse, Billy Williams, Sid Hogg

Bentham Football Club
'Parkinson Collegian Cup Winners' **1976**
Back Row left to right D. Hogg, T. Newhouse, D. Lumb, Mayor (Cllr. W. Joel), C. Quinn, N. Taylor, P. Waddington, T. Dawber (the secretary).
Front Row left to right J. Winn, D. Wadeson, R.Russell, N. Corrigan (Captain), D. MacLennan, M. Brown, K. Thompson (Mascot)
(Photo W. Heigh)

Low Bentham Football Club 1949/1950
Back Row left to right J.Burrow, G. Downham, D Birks, W. Cochrane, Jack Bibby, Jim Coates.
Front Row left to right Colin Wilcock, D Slinger, …………?, Watson Cornthwaite, (president) Ron Tomlinson, W. Vickers, Albert Coates, Ed. Downham
(Photo V. Lawson)

Bentham Second Eleven Cricket Team about 1948
Back Row G. Downham, Albert Burrow, R. Guy, F. Bibby, B. Cowgill, F. Forster, G. Slinger, Kath Downham.
Front Row T. Blondel, B. Magoolagan, A. Patrickson, H. Lister, ...?

This picture was taken earlier when a visiting team from Nelson played at Bentham on 3rd April 1946. Notice (extreme left, front row) Y.B. Palwanker, an Indian *'pro'* who later played for Lancaster Cricket Club, and (front row, third from the left) Learie Constantine, Nelson's professional, still revered in Nelson and Lancashire cricketing circles. He was later knighted, then, as *'Baron Constantine of Maraval and Nelson'* became High Commissioner for Trinidad and Tobago. After the match he presented John Fisher with a clock bearing the date mentioned above.
(Photos C. Fisher)

The Green Smithy Harvest was held in Fred Heseltine's garage at the Green Smithy between 1950 and 1956. It was started by Mrs. Robert Taylor and was an auction of harvest produce to raise funds for the R.N.I.B. Richard Turner was usually the auctioneer with the help of Bill Joel. One such harvest display is shown and the large group (below) with the minister in the centre shows a gathering before an auction. *(Photo Wendy Heigh)*

Methodism in Bentham has a long proud history. The first chapel in High Bentham was built in 1820 on the Main Street, at Wesley Place. The Methodist Church on Station Road was built in 1905 when larger and improved accommodation became a necessity.

The Methodists struggled to establish themselves in Low Bentham. Early attempts in the 1830s and 1850s fizzled and it was not until the 1880s that more regular services were held in the harness room at Lake House and eventually on January 2nd 1886 the foundation stone was laid for Low Bentham Chapel. This photograph shows a group gathered outside High Bentham Methodist Church on 20th November 1955. **Back Row** Mrs Paley, Pauline Cowin, Pat Shuttleworth, Bunty Crawford, Vera Hutchinson

Amongst those on the front row are: Janet Metcalfe, the Ellershaw girls, John Towler, Christopher Calverley, Janet & Christopher Clapham, Barry Clapham, Brian Ralston and Robin Towler. *(Photo Caralyn Simpson)*

The winter of 1947 was long and hard. It commenced early in late January and lasted until Easter. Dr. Dowell said he could visit his patients by walking in a direct line over the fields and over the hedges that were buried by the snow.

The photographs show Low Bentham during that winter. There is a picture of Tim Houldsworth's car against a snow drift on Doctor's Hill, and two of Low Bentham Main Street. *(Photos B. Ellershaw)*

This interesting picture was taken from Queen's Square, Low Bentham (outside the Victoria Institute). It shows the view looking East up Bentham Road towards High Bentham about 1900. The road, far removed from today's busy thoroughfare, has the rural aspect of a country lane. *(Photo The Howson Collection)*

The road was widened and improved about 1936. The *'Lancaster Guardian'* of 24th August 1934 states *'After years of waiting, planning and scheming it would seem that at long last the narrow road between High and Low Bentham, which in places is only wide enough to allow the passage of one vehicle, is to be widened at an estimated cost of £14,000…it is anticipated that the work will begin in the autumn as the scheme is seventh on the list…at one point the road is only twelve feet wide. There is no footpath although the road is used very frequently by pedestrians.'* In November 1938 the children of the schools of both High and Low Bentham planted about two thousand daffodil bulbs on the banks at the approaches to both settlements. The photograph shows Miss Clark and the High Bentham pupils planting bulbs on the bank near High Bentham. *(Photo School Collection)*

The cross at Low Bentham was constructed in 1902 to mark the coronation of Edward VII. It is said that the villagers placed a time capsule beneath the cross before they started construction. It is made of concrete and was moulded around a barrel to make the base. A downspout was the base for the upright. Those seeing the cross in 2007 will notice that a small section at its top is missing. The photograph was taken about 1910 *(Photo E. Willan)*

This picture shows Low Bentham Cooperative Society's shop about 1904. The area at this time was known as Queens Square.

The shop opened in 1891 and closed in 1960. For many years this area has been known as '*Co-op Corner*'. The right hand window as you face the shop features a display of men's and children's clothes while the other window has a beautifully arranged window display of bottles, possibly containing sauces and soft drinks. The man to the extreme right appears to be leaning against the window bottom with a basket against his legs and a spaniel dog sitting on the basket. There were several shops in the village at that time including a bakery, a butcher's, a post office, a grocer's, a greengrocer's, a newsagent and general stores. The presence of a landau with its coachman gives the impression that the man standing immediately to its right could be a person of some importance in the community but we have no clue to his identity. It is just possible, however, that he is Robert Garnett of The Ridding. According to the 1891 census he was '*living on his own means*'. He had a wife, Alice, a son Robert, five servants and a coachman called Richard Preston who lived at the Lodge. *(Photo E. Duesbury)*

This fine photograph shows Burton Road (also called *'Doctor's Hill'* and once *'Lake House Hill'*), Low Bentham, in about 1910. The children, some in their 'Sunday best' clothes break off from their games to pose for the man setting up his camera on a tripod – something still a rare sight. The photographer was

Mr. T. Turner from Skipton, who turned his photographs into picture postcards that would then cost a half-penny to post. Apart from the addition of the occasional porch the appearance of Cheapside has changed very little in a century. The land to the west, on the hill was not developed for a further 60 years. *(Photo Helen Fleming)*

This view was probably taken in about 1925 from the bank overlooking Ford Ayrton's Silk Mill. The signal box, signal, coal heaps and the siding for the coal wagons are visible as is Longlands Farm. *(Photo Helen Fleming)*

Prior to 1904, all Low Bentham village functions were limited to accommodation available in two venues, the Parochial School or a reading room on Main Street in a cottage somewhere near Bridge House. The idea for a village institute was first mooted in about 1880 and a subscription list was opened. To mark Queen Victoria's Diamond Jubilee in 1897, the committee received a substantial gift from a local person and subscriptions from Benthamers all over the world. Building took place during 1904 and the hall was opened on 24th February 1905 by Thomas Armistead Foxcroft (the architect) and Thomas Benson Pease Ford (the owner of Ford, Ayrton Silk Mill). The curious wooden hut protruding out into the road belonged to George Parker, the village hairdresser. *(Photo W.P. Howson)*

The hall seems to have played a major part in village life for some time but during the Second World War the building had minimal use because in 1940 West Riding County Council introduced a school meals kitchen there. The photograph shows the kitchen staff in about 1950. They are:
Back Row Amy Wilson, Miss Pearson
Middle Row Nellie Tallon, Maggie Maunders, Dorothy Lang
Front Row Alice Slinger, Martha Ellershaw *(Photo Mary Parker)*
After the kitchens closed, the Institute was refurbished and it re-opened in August 1988.

Low Bentham was a close-knit, busy village with the majority of community life revolving around work at Ford Ayrton Mill, the two schools, church, chapel, the Institute and the public houses. The following photographs illustrate some aspects of that life. On this page there is a picture taken about 1915 showing the mill girls returning home *(Photo M. Sharp)* and St John The Baptist Church Mothers' Union in about 1930 *(Photo Rhoda Coates)*. Members of the Mothers' Union shown are:

Back Row Mrs Fletcher (of Crow Trees), Canon Garrard, Mrs Bownass, Mrs Nelly Tomlinson
Second Row from Back Mrs Jane Townson, Mrs Walling, Mrs Alice Coates, Mrs Clara Downham, Mrs Priscilla Jennings, Mrs Lee, Mrs Polly Burrows, ...?, Mrs Phillipson (Oysterber Farm), ...?, Mrs Mabel Robinson
Sitting On Chairs Mrs Ada Robinson, ...?, Mrs Willan, Mrs Garrad, Mrs Walters, Mrs Prince, Mrs Norcross, Mrs Nat. Burrows, Mrs Dodgson (Lake House)
Front Row Mrs Rebecca Downham, Mrs Agnes Marshall, Mrs Alice Oldfield, Mrs Elsie Oldfield *(Photo Rhoda Coates)*

During the 1930s, community spirit was strong in Low Bentham, shown by the drama productions staged by the Parish Church Mothers' Union. Husbands and wives participated and the Bentham Orchestra accompanied the plays. The productions were staged in the Victoria Institute and were enjoyed by large audiences.

Low Bentham Mothers' Union Play *'Love in The Alps'* 1932
Back Row Ada Downham, Mr H. Coates, Mr J. Lister, Mrs Alice Coates, Mr Robert Downham
Middle Row Arnold Robinson, Mrs Walters, Mr Percy Wilcock, Clara Downham, Mrs Alice Burrow
Front Row Mrs. Lee, Mrs Agnes Marshall, Mrs Becca Downham, Mrs Jane Townson, Kathy Brown, (on ground), Mrs. Phillipson. *(Photo The David Johnson Collection)*

Low Bentham Parish Mothers' Union Play *'Doctors Orders'* 1937
Back Row E. Downham, Mrs Jennings, Minnie Coates, Ada Robinson, Polly Burrow, Arthur Jennings, Isobel Atkinson, Alice Coates, Agnes Marshall, Ben Coates
Front Row Arnold Robinson, Mrs Maunders, Alice Burrow, Percy Wilcock, Mrs Walters, Jane Townson, Mrs Rebecca Downham, Bob Downham. *(Photo The David Johnson Collection)*

For many years there were two primary schools in Low Bentham. There was the Parochial School on Main Street and the County Primary School on Burton Road. The Parochial School opened in 1849 and closed 131 years later in 1980. Low Bentham C.P. School opened in 1909. It was built under the 'Hundred Thousand Grant' of 1907 under which education authorities could open a 'secular' school in villages where more than 30 children petitioned for a school to be built. The West Riding County Council received a petition from 62 parents at Low Bentham.

The top photograph shows the Junior class at the County Primary School in 1950

Back Row Keith Parker, George Jackson, Ted Bitchell, Ted Lang, Margaret Bruce, Bob Burns, Bernard Ellershaw, Andrew Hawkins, Alan Proctor.

Middle Row Ingrid Bell, Rose Parker, Julie Burns, Ann Burns, Mary Dixon, Joan Craddock, Edwina Bibby, Barbara Craddock.

Front Row Roy Wilkinson, Robert Orton, Alban Burns (*Photo B. Ellershaw*)

Low Bentham C.P. School 1956
Back Row Joe Lawson, David Wilcock, Reg Errington, Ken Proctor, Ian Ross, Melvyn Louth, Trevor Wheildon
Middle Row Debbie William, Jackie Wrathall, Patsy Lister, Pauline Field, Angela Harrison, Pauline Slinger, Doris Bell.
Front Row Jean Lister, Belinda Parnell, Mary Burrow, Kathryn Harrison.
    (*Photo The David Johnson Collection*)

A view of the Main Street featuring Low Bentham Parochial School and taken about 1900.
(Photo The Howson Collection)

Taken in 1977, this picture shows the children of the Parochial School gathered in the schoolyard after a road safety lesson from the police. On the left is Colin Garner, the Headteacher and just left of centre Mrs. Ann Whitaker (assistant teacher). Behind is the outline of Brook Cottage, once the home of the Ford family. The school closed in 1980 and became the Evaglades Home. *(Photo The David Johnson Collection)*

Low Bentham Parochial School in about 1954
Staff left to Right Mrs Tomlinson, Miss Robinson, Miss Pearson and Mrs Preston
Each table starting at the front left and working backwards and round to the front right (some flexibility may be needed in the interpretation!) :
Left hand table: R. Priestley, S. Watson, K. Tomlinson, S. Jennings, H. Cross, M. Dodgson, R. Turner, S. Cornthwaite, N. Wright, R. Turner, P.J. Coates, Katherine Hope, …..? *Standing* P. Wright, Betty Baines
Middle Table: C. Reid, G. Wright, T. Armstrong, D. Ramwell, A. Clapham, R. Cornthwaite, M. Slee, D. Taylor, A. Coates, S. Hinde, J. Brayshaw, E. Coates, L. Ely. *Standing* H. Slee, Y Slee?, D. Brayshaw, L. Brayshaw, J.D. Preston, J. Brayshaw?, …..?
Right Hand Table: A. Priestley, A. Coates, P. Slinger, Susan Russell, S.Roe, S. Foster, J. Armstrong, L.Capstick, J. Wellington, D. Burrow *(Photo Mrs B. Armstrong)*

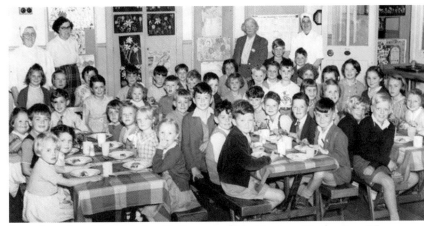

Low Bentham Parochial School 1951
Back Row …..?, Francis Hardy Burt, John Skeats, Michael Pridmore, Michael Walling, Eric Clay, Terry Hodgson
Third Row Doug Taylor, Keith Watkinson, Michael Mason, John Brayshaw, Ronnie Fleming, Billy Slee, Ken Pearson, Geoff Tidsley, Brian Slee
Second Row Heather Slee, …..?, Sheila Cornthwaite, Hazel Cross, Joan Wilson, Dorothy Mason, Doreena Crayston, Joyce Thornber, Eileen Ramwell, Carol Hind, Sylvia Fleming, Judith Wellington, Marjorie Dodgson
Front Row Susan Hardy Burt, Margaret Willan, Celia Ramwell *(Photo Keith Watkinson)*

The Education Act of 1870 was a vital step in bringing universal education to all children but it presented a problem for Bentham because there was a lack of suitable accommodation. When 'Moonsacre' came up for sale in 1878 the Grammar School governors quickly agreed to buy the premises for £1160 and it became home to Bentham Grammar School. The main building was given over to accommodation for the headmaster and the boarders but immediately after the purchase the governors erected a schoolroom with a gallery. In 1948 it moved once more to the Rectory at Low Bentham (now the site of Sedbergh Junior School).

The top picture shows Moonsacre in about 1930 and below it is a photograph of the staff and scholars about 1932 or 1933.

They are:

Back Row P. Wright, ...?, R. Bowker, ? Sanderson, ...?, T. Davey, B. Marshall, J. Seggar, ...? Arthur Ammatt.

Next to the Back Row N. Robinson, ...?, E Bateson, ...?, R. Garlick, G. Slater, D. Bond, W. Atkinson, ...?, ...?

Second Row W. Park, H. Bush, ?Ellison, P. Booth, G.P. Gill (Headmaster), T. Woods, C. Garlick, ...?, ...?

Front Row ? Burrows, B. Bowness, ...?, ...?,........?,.......?, B. Foster, T. Burrows.

(Photos H. Garlick)

Lord Baden Powell founded the scouting movement in 1907 after a camping trip on Brownsea Island. This picture taken in about 1917 at Moonsacre must be the first picture of a scout troop in Bentham. Although most of the boys are holding staffs the leader (in the centre) and the boy to his right appear to be holding rifles, suggesting a military perspective to this First World War picture. There are no records of the troop but it must have died out in the early part of the twentieth century. Scouting at the school was revived for a brief period in the 1990s.
(Photo Bentham Grammar School Archives)

The school underwent considerable expansion from 1927 onwards and was remodelled to provide improved teaching, dining and boarding accomodation. The new building seen in the lower picture was opened on 26th April 1928. Local pupils and students from a distance who *'boarded'* were educated at the school.
(Photo The David Johnson Collection)

Between 1920 and 1937 George Percy Gill was headmaster of Bentham Grammar School. His wife Mathilde was German and played a major part in catering at the school. She was also a fine swimmer and taught many people in Bentham to swim. She conducted her swimming lessons in the River Wenning at 6.00 a.m. The lessons were held variously at Camp Hole, near the Wenning Oak, at Winder Wheel and in the 'cut', the millrace that fed the turbines at Ford, Ayrton Silk Mill.

The photographs show Mrs Gill teaching swimming. In the upper photograph she is using the 'cut' with branches spanning the water and ropes attached to the branches to help the boys as they trod water against the current. (Photos Mrs E.Tyrer)

The earliest school badge appeared when the school was located at Moonsacre. In those days it was simply a lozenge with a crescent and the date of the school's foundation (1726). The crescent had a dual meaning referring to both 'moonsacre' and the bends in the River Wenning. The badge was formalised during Mr. Webb's time in the 1950s when the school moved to Low Bentham. The two wavy lines represent the confluence of the River Wenning and Eskerbeck and the motto 'Surgam' meaning 'I shall arise'.